I0110507

The Most Beautiful

BLANK NOTEBOOK

AND JOURNAL, KEEP TRACK OF EVERYTHING

Activinotes

Activinotes

DAILY JOURNALS, PLANNERS, NOTEBOOKS AND OTHER BLANK BOOKS

This Book Belongs To

____

Today

Things to do

Notes

Today

Things to do

Notes

Today

Things to do

Notes

Today

Things to do

Notes

Today

Things to do

Notes

Today

Things to do

Notes

Today

Things to do

Notes

Today

Things to do

Notes

Today

Things to do

Notes

Today

Things to do

Notes

Today

Things to do

Notes

Today

Things to do

Notes

Today

Things to do

Notes

Today

Things to do

Notes

Today

Things to do

Notes

Today

Things to do

Notes

Today

Things to do

Notes

Today

Things to do

Notes

Today

Things to do

Notes

Today

Things to do

Notes

Today

Things to do

Notes

Today

Things to do

Today

Things to do

Notes

Today

Things to do

Notes

Today

Things to do

Notes

Today

Things to do

Notes

Today

Things to do

Notes

Today

Things to do

Notes

Today

Things to do

Notes

Today

Things to do

Notes

Today

Things to do

Notes

Today

www.ingramcontent.com/pod-product-compliance
Lightning Source LLC
Chambersburg PA
CBHW081337090426
42737CB00017B/3187
* 9 7 8 1 6 8 3 2 1 8 7 2 2 *